THE MYSTERIOUS

BUG

KATE SIMKINS

ILLUSTRATED BY JAMES WARWOOD

This is a work of fiction. Names, characters, places, and incidents either are the product of the author's imagination or are used fictitiously. Any resemblance to actual persons, living or dead, events, or locales is entirely coincidental.

Big Thinking Publishing, Hoole House Barn, PR3 0JE

First paperback edition March 2025

Cover, Illustrations & Interior Design by James Warwood
Edited by Daniel Mills

ISBN: 978-1-0683099-0-8

To my extraordinary daughters, Harriet and Alice.

May your lives be filled with wonder.

CHAPTER ONE

MEET BUG

Now, you might think that Bug is a cute little bundle of loveliness, and while this is mostly true, it is not *always* the case. You see, Bug has an **AMAZING** ability to get into all sorts of troubles and scrapes. Another important thing to know about our Bug is that he really, really likes a chat. Unless, of course, he is in his little jar. By the way, please don't feel upset about

him being in his jar, because he is really, *really* happy in there. In fact, he carries it around in his little shoulder bag for when he needs a nap. And the reason he puts it in his bag is because it is too big to fit into his pocket. I asked him, once, how he could possibly *fit* the jar into such a small bag, but he gave me such a withering look, and made me feel so silly for asking, that I didn't bother to ask again.

When Bug is in his jar, we can all breathe a huge sigh of relief, because we can pretty much guarantee that nothing is going to go catastrophically wrong while he is in there. (There was one blissful time when he stayed in his jar for *two whole days,* but that was because he had been telling me the story of when he once lived with a brontosaurus, and it was quite a long tale. It took *three full weeks* to tell, and we were both exhausted by the end. I look back at those two days quite fondly. *Sigh.*)

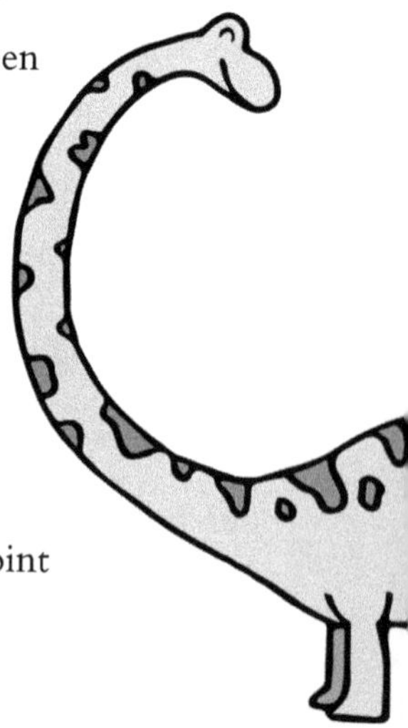

This brings me to the next important point

about our Bug, and I shall whisper it to you, in case he overhears. You cannot always be sure that he is telling the truth. Did you hear? Sorry, let me try again. I said...

YOU CANNOT ALWAYS BE SURE THAT HE IS TELLING THE TRUTH.

Oh crumbs, now I've done it. But in all fairness, the few times I have called him out on a very, *very* obvious lie (much more than just a little fib), he didn't even have the decency to look sheepish. Now I think that's because our Bug isn't trying to be mean or deceitful… it's just that he has told his stories so many times that he *believes* them to be true, which means that he isn't technically lying. Do you get what I mean?

But I have been doing my research, and I'm pretty sure that the tales I am going to tell you now all happened *more or less* as Bug says they did. He has been pestering and mithering for ages for me to

write them down, because his thumbs don't work the same way that ours do, and so here they are.

The first story I am going to tell you is very, very important, because it sets off a whole chain of events that no one, not even our Bug, could have foreseen. It will also give you a chance to get to know our Bug a bit so, by the end, you might be able to tell which bits of the story are true and which bits he may have made up. But before we start, I can give you a clue… if the disaster turns out to be Bug's fault, chances are the tale is true. If Bug comes away from the story looking squeaky clean and innocent, he has probably changed the ending.

So. Are you sitting comfortably? Then let us begin. Our first story starts with Bug swimming in the lovely warm waters of the

Mediterranean Sea. If you don't know your geography too well, this is the big bit of water around Greece and Italy, and places like that. Bug is a brilliant swimmer because, underneath all the fluff and nonsense, he has a huge pair of slightly webbed feet.

As Bug was swimming along, quite happily, he happened to run into an old friend, Harry the dolphin. Harry's full name was Harriet, but as we all know, dolphins like to shorten people's names. I once asked a dolphin why they bother giving long names to their children if they are just going to shorten them anyway, but as I don't speak echo, I couldn't be sure of their response.

It's actually quite a funny coincidence that I don't speak echo, because neither does Bug, but he had always wanted to learn, whereas I can't be bothered. So it was lucky that Harriet knew how to speak English, because if she hadn't, she wouldn't have been able to invite Bug for tea, and that would have been a *disaster*. Why's that such a big deal? Let me explain.

As you probably already know, manners are super, *super* important to dolphins. They are remarkably hospitable and will feel ashamed if they don't ask you to share a beverage. So if Harry hadn't spoken English, she might have found herself kicked out of the pod, which would have been *awful*. But that didn't happen. So *phew*! What Harriet *did* do, because she is super lovely, was check with her parents whether Bug could join in at Dolphin School (Grade 2) and learn to speak properly.

Of course, the answer was "yes", and so Bug soon found himself with his own little underwater desk in the Grade 2 classroom. Even though Bug wasn't keen on school on land, he found that school underwater was actually quite enjoyable (even if there was a dolphin behind him that kept kicking his chair all the time). At playtime, Bug and Harry would swim out to sea and play with the turtles, but towards the end of the third week of Dolphin School, Bug spotted something.

A boat.

And an island.

And some dodgy-looking guys with something big and heavy.

Now, if Bug had ears, they would have pricked up at that

point, like a dog's. But he doesn't, so they didn't. Despite that, Bug realised that he had stumbled across his next adventure.

The idea of treasure was almost overwhelming for Bug (as he is incredibly attracted to shiny things), so he said goodbye to Harry and her pod, promising to email soon and tell them all about his adventures, and set off after the boat.

As Bug approached the island, his hopes were confirmed. There *was* a chest, and surely it contained plenty of things that sparkle and shine. *Treasure?* Bug thought to himself. *Lovely.*

CHAPTER TWO

A PAIR OF (POTENTIAL) PIRATES

Bug floated over to the tiny island and waited in the shallows to figure out what was happening. The beach was lovely and sandy, but it had a few (rather helpful) big rocks that were a perfect hiding spot for our Bug. It wasn't long before he heard two rather loud voices approaching.

"Pull it my way, you idiot!" said Voice One.

"NO! Bring it my way!" argued Voice Two.

Interesting, thought Bug.

"Who brought you along anyway?" grumbled Voice One.

answered Voice Two.

Bug giggled, as he'd always liked the word "wazzock". Whoever these two miscreants were, they were clearly not getting along.

"I've had about enough of you!" shouted Voice One.

"Well, off you go then, and I'll keep all this loot for myself!" Voice Two shouted back.

Now Bug was *really* interested. *Treasure confirmed,* he thought. Now, I mentioned before that Bug liked shiny things, but I'm not sure I really explained what *sort* of shiny things Bug likes the best.

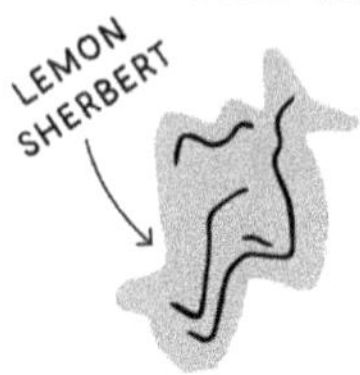

When normal people (like you and me) think of treasure, we think of gold and silver and other precious things like that. But not our Bug. Oh no.

At this point in the story, Bug was imagining himself with loads and loads *and loads* of rolls of tinfoil. Or at least those sweet wrappers that are coloured, but you can still see through them. Do you know the ones I mean? Oh, and chewing gum wrappers! He loves those, too. Do you know, I once caught Bug Sellotaping those sweet wrappers up inside his little jar and it was actually quite beautiful. A bit like a stained glass window… but I digress. Sorry.

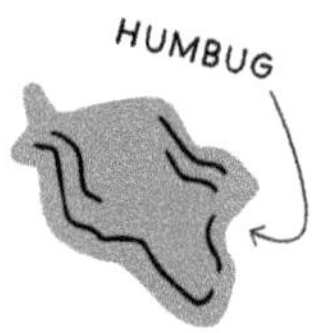

So. Bug's initial hopes and dreams were confirmed, and he now knew for *definite* that he was dealing with treasure. He peeped over his rock, and looked for himself. Sure enough, the two men were hauling a heavy-looking chest out of

the boat and up towards the trees.

Bug thought for a moment about the two gentlemen on the beach. He was *almost* certain that they were **REAL-LIFE PIRATES**, although he couldn't be totally sure. Voice One did have a wooden leg and a parrot on his shoulder, and Voice Two had a bandana and an eye patch, but Bug didn't want to make any judgements. (He is quite good like that.) As he settled in for a bit of a wait, he dug around in his little shoulder bag for a snack. As I am sure you know, Bug's most favourite of favourite snacks is a cheese and pickle sandwich, and happily, he found the remains of one squished into a corner at the bottom of his bag. Taking it out, he picked off the bits of fluff and mould, and munched quite happily as he watched and waited.

Despite the sandwich, Bug was getting more and more excited as he watched the pair of (potential) pirates heaving their chest and some digging tools up the shoreline. He already knew that once the (potential) pirates had left, he was going to dig up the treasure and see what was inside. *It's not stealing if it's already*

stolen, he thought. (Questionable morals, readers, questionable morals.)

It took quite a while for the guys to finish the job, but when they were finally done, they sat down and opened a bottle that had R-U-M spelled out in big letters on the label. Now, as Bug can't read, he had no idea what that could *possibly* mean, but when the bottle was empty, the two men walked back to their rowing boat in a rather wobbly fashion.

As soon as the (potential) pirates had rowed out of sight, Bug called to the birds that lived on the little island. Now, we know that Bug is exceedingly good at languages, and once he had worked out the *species* of the birds, he found that he could communicate with them quite fluently. The birds agreed to lend a hand, and explained that the price of their help would be whatever was left over once Bug had taken *his* share of the shiny things. A contract was drawn up, and before long, both parties had signed it and they were ready to start digging.

Happily, the birds had enormously long, strong

beaks, which they used to break open the coconuty-style nuts that grew on the island, so the soft sand was no bother at all for them to dig through. Bug helped by digging with his big feet, and within a few minutes, they had uncovered the chest.

Getting the chest out of the hole was a bit trickier, but the birds formed a separate task force and soon had the answer. Ropes were fashioned out of the palm tree leaves and, with a little bit of heaving and ho-ing, they managed to put the ropes underneath the treasure chest. The birds grasped the ropes in their beaks and flew upwards, and slowly, slowly, the chest was air-lifted out of the hole. High fives were exchanged (if you can call it that, using wings and feet and the like) before they settled down to open the chest.

Bug excitedly lifted the lid, for once using his hands instead of his enormous feet, and once he had gotten over his disappointment at there not being any *immediately visible* rolls of tinfoil, he realised that he was looking at something very special indeed. Lifting a large red stone out of the chest, he held it to the light and was hypnotised by the sparkle. *Lovely*, he thought. *Gems*.

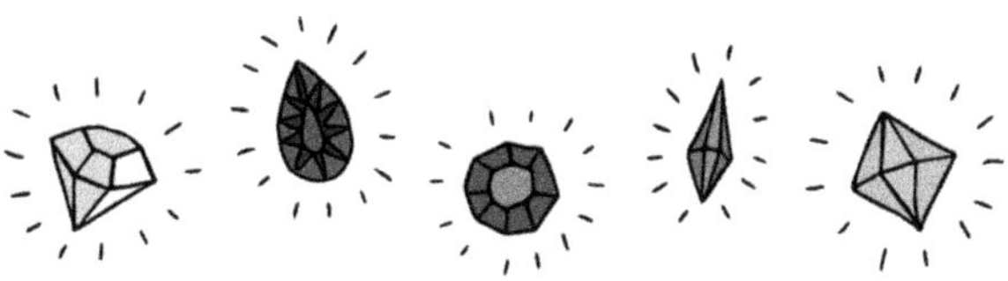

CHAPTER THREE

THE STOLEN GEMS

So. Here is where we stand. Bug is on his lovely desert island, and in his possession are fifteen (stolen by the potential pirates) beautiful Gems. What Bug *didn't* know at this point, but what I will tell you, because I know I can trust you, is that these were not ordinary Gems. Oh no. These were *Dragon* Gems.

Now, you may have figured out that Bug is not always the cleverest of creatures, and he was about to make his most catastrophic decision yet. Bug was transfixed by the special Gems and secretly thought that they were *miles* better than tinfoil, based on the shiny factor alone. Plus, he could see through them, just like his sweet wrappers. *Bonus*, he thought.

However, at this point, Bug did something that I was quite proud of him for. I was so pleased and surprised, in fact, that when he got to this part of the story, my hand jerked and I drew a big black line through all of my writing and had to start the page again. You see, Bug decided not to take *ALL* of the Gems. Do you see how grown up of him that was? In times past, Bug would have taken them all, consequences be damned, but this time, he only took five, leaving ten behind. *This way*, Bug thought proudly,

THE OWNERS WOULD GET BACK MOST OF THEIR GEMS!

Are you proud of him too?

Of course the birds *could* have taken the rest of the Gems, as agreed in their contract, but they dismissed them for not having quite the right amount of sparkle, so the ten remaining Gems stayed in the chest.

Plan made, Bug was ready to move on to his next adventure,

but then he did something really, *really* stupid. He left the owners of the treasure a note, written by one of his new bird friends.

And then he had the bird draw a little picture of him, so the dragons would know what he looked like.

I am sure you are sighing with disbelief at the idiocy of Bug's plan, but he was totally happy and felt very pleased about his cleverness. After thanking the birds, Bug headed back into the water to get away from the island before the Gems' owners came back.

He swam south for a while, before noticing a harbour. He surfaced to see a beautiful white city on the side of a mountain, leading down to the sea. He stared for a moment in disbelief – some of the buildings were topped with gold, and oh, how they sparkled! Feeling as though he had found his spiritual home, Bug swam to the shore and climbed out onto a little beach, much to the surprise of two passing girls, who had never seen anything quite like Bug before!

They got a little more than they had bargained for, however, when Bug shook himself like a dog and soaked them both from head to toe. As he brushed the fluff from his eyes, he did a double-take. He was seeing double!

One of the girls laughed. "It's okay, it's not you, we're twins!"

Bug was surprised to find that he could understand them perfectly. *Maybe they are speaking dolphin,* he thought. He shrugged. Bug's grasp of languages was so good, he could barely remember which was which, and it didn't bother him at all that he had no idea what language he was speaking. Not one bit.

"Hello, twins. I'm Bug."

"It's lovely to meet you. I'm Elizabeth…"

"And I'm Alice," finished the other twin.

"Bug is a funny name!" said Elizabeth. (Not unkindly, she was just surprised.)

"My real name is far too long and complicated to explain! And it's lovely to meet you too." Bug looked around. "But *where* am I meeting you?"

"This," Alice gestured all around her, "is the city of Atlantis!"

"Goodness!" replied Bug. "I didn't realise I had swam that far! It's rather beautiful."

"Thank you," said Elizabeth, proudly. "Would you like a little tour? We don't get visitors too often."

Bug nodded enthusiastically and followed the girls around the city. They passed market stalls selling everything from delicious-looking foods to fossilised dragon eggs.

As they walked, Bug told them all about his adventures, right up to the point where he had found the Gems.

"What kind of Gems?" asked Alice, curiously.

"Would you like to see?"

The girls nodded and Bug rummaged around in his bag, throwing out items left, right and centre.

"Aha!" Bug proudly pulled out his prize, and the girl's faces went very, very pale.

"Did you take that, Bug?" Elizabeth asked.

"Yes, but I left most of them behind," answered Bug, proudly. "Would you like to see the rest of them?"

"No!" Shouted both of the girls at once. (Twins often say

things at the same time… have you noticed that about twins?)

"What is it? What's wrong?"

The twins exchanged a glance. "I think we had better take you to our mum," said Elizabeth. "She will know what to do."

With a sinking feeling in his tummy, Bug followed the girls up a cobbled street to a tall house that was squished in amongst a lot of smaller ones. There was a sign on the door that Bug couldn't read, but I will tell you what it said anyway, as it is important. The sign read "Dragon Chaser" in big, gold letters. Even though he couldn't read the sign, Bug knew where he was going because, as well as the words, there was an enormous picture of a dragon… a dragon guarding gems just like the ones in his bag. He gulped. *Maybe this time*, he thought, *I have gotten in over my head.*

CHAPTER FOUR

THE "ACCIDENT" AT ATLANTIS

The twins and Bug entered the house and Bug stared around in amazement. It was a treasure trove! The walls were hung with maps, ancient-looking weapons, and more than one shiny thing that Bug wanted desperately to have for himself.

They made their way into what looked to be an office, and behind a heavy, wooden desk was Elizabeth's and Alice's mum… The Dragon Chaser of Atlantis.

The Dragon Chaser was quite small for a human. She had short, curly brown hair and a nasty-looking scar down one cheek. Bug stood looking at his feet as the twins filled their mum in on what Bug had told them. At least *this* time, he managed to look a little bit sorry.

As the twins were talking, a man appeared in the doorway holding a tray full of mugs. "Tea?" He offered. "And how about a sandwich?"

This man suddenly became Bug's *most favourite* human in the *whole world.*

"Cheese and pickle?" Bug asked, hopefully.

The man smiled, kindly. "Of course."

"Ham for me!" The twins said, at exactly the same time. "Thanks, Dad!"

As the twins finished their tale, their mum sighed deeply. *Maybe she's tired*, thought Bug.

"Right," said Katarina (because that was her name). "So you have some Dragon Gems?"

Bug nodded uncomfortably, feeling as though he might be in trouble. (You know that feeling when you're about to be told off for something? You know, when someone uses your *full name?* That's how

Bug was feeling, right at this moment.)

"May I see?" asked Katarina, gently.

Bug wriggled off his shoulder bag and the twins gasped as Katarina lifted out the gems. They really were incredibly beautiful.

Katarina looked carefully at Bug. "Did you know what they were when you took them, Bug?"

Bug shook his head.

"Have you had dealings with dragons before?"

Bug shook his head again.

"Ever met one?"

Bug paled, which made him go a strange shade of grey. He shook his head again.

"Well, then. At least you didn't do it on purpose." She looked at the twins. "You know what to do."

The twins left the room just as their Dad reappeared in the doorway.

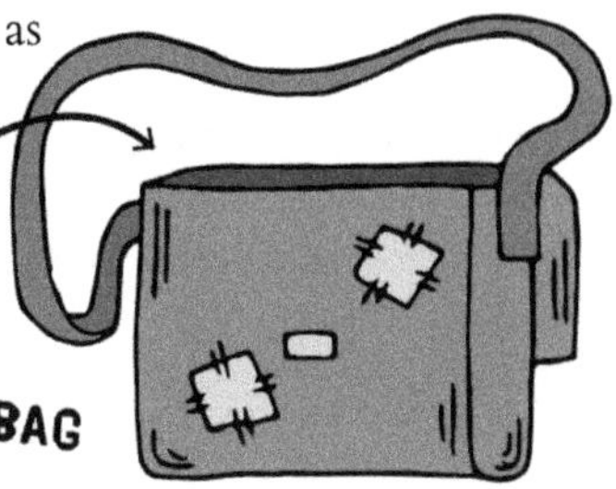

BUG'S SHOULDER BAG

"One cheese and pickle, two ha…. oh! Where did they go?"

"To raise the alarm," replied Katarina.

"Oh dear, oh dear. Righty-oh then. Fancy a sandwich, Kat?"

She reached over and took one. "Might be a while 'till we get food again," she mumbled through a mouthful of butty.

"What's going to happen?" asked Bug, cautiously. He wasn't entirely sure he wanted to know the answer.

"We have a difficult relationship with dragons," said Katarina, between bites. "Every once in a while they come and try to take the gold from the tops of the building. It's my job to try and stop them. Every generation has a Dragon Chaser, and when I pass on the role, for the first time ever there will be two Chasers in Atlantis."

"Because they are twins!" exclaimed Bug.

"Exactly. I've kept the dragons away for years, but now, thanks to you, they have a reason to come back."

"Because I brought the Gems." Bug looked down at his feet again, a little ashamed.

"So now we must raise the alarm, shut down the city, and get everyone to where they are safest. The boats."

"Is there anything I can do?" asked Bug, rightly feeling

somewhat responsible.

"No, Bug, not right now."

Katarina left Bug to his cheese and pickle sandwich and went to deal with the chaos and carnage that he had managed to create.

Now, I don't want you to feel like Bug is uncaring about the messes that he makes, he just doesn't really *understand* in the same way you or I would. And it is virtually *impossible* for Bug to feel bad or sad when he is eating a cheese and pickle sandwich. By the time he had finished this one (which I believe was a truly exceptional example of the genre), Bug's guilt had faded away and he was back to being his normal, cheerful self.

After taking his plate to the kitchen and washing up the mugs (it was the least he could do), Bug left the house and wandered back down to the harbour, doing his best to cheer people up as they were running for their lives. As he approached the harbour wall, he watched Alice and Elizabeth help the people of Atlantis onto their boats. They spotted him and beckoned him over.

“Come on, Bug. Hop on this little boat here and we’ll join you. Look, here’s Dad now.”

The twins’ dad climbed aboard (carrying a little backpack that Bug had high hopes contained a sandwich or two), and finally, Katarina joined them, having been to check the city was empty.

The boats bobbed around for a little while until suddenly, on the horizon, Bug spotted a black cloud approaching the island. He tugged at Katarina’s tunic and pointed.

“And so it begins,” she whispered.

As the dragons approached, their wings caused a huge tidal wave that made Bug understand why all Atlanteans had access to the boats. He watched in horror as the tidal wave covered the whole city.

The largest of the dragons came to a mid-air stop, right above the twins’ boat (which was actually quite an impressive thing to achieve), and he looked down at Bug angrily. The dragon was huge, his pearly-white scales glinting in the sunlight.

“GEMS. NOW,” the dragon demanded, and Bug sheepishly handed over four of the gems, leaving one still stashed in his bag.

"That's all I have. I dropped one while I was swimming."

Now, you and me both know that this is not true, because I would have told you if Bug had dropped a Gem. What we have here is another example of Bug not telling the truth. Now I'm telling you this story as it happened, without hiding any of the rubbish bits, because I feel that I can trust you *not* to copy our naughty Bug. You and I *both* know that stealing is *very, very bad* and that Bug should be totally ashamed of himself and tell the truth. This did not happen, however, and I am afraid to say that he stuck with his massive fib.

Bug handed over the four (not five) Gems, and the dragon turned to Katarina.

"Chaser, nice to see you again."

"And you, Prince Grane of the White Dragon Reaches. Now, will you please leave my city?"

Prince Grane grinned, which looked entirely ferocious, truth be told, and then he turned tail and flew away, the rest of the dragons following in his wake.

"When will you be able to go back to the city?" asked Bug quietly, for the flood waters were still covering the island.

"Soon. The waters will recede, they always do," answered

Katarina with a small smile. "I think we have managed to avert disaster. Next time, young Bug," Katarina looked at him quite seriously, "could you let us know when you are coming? That way we will have time to prepare."

Bug didn't really notice the tone of Katarina's voice, and took her comment to mean that all was well and everything was totally fine.

"Course I will!" he said. "I'll drop you an email!" And with that, Bug hopped off the side of the boat and into the water, waving at Alice and Elizabeth before disappearing under the waves.

Elizabeth waved back, shaking her head in disbelief at the whole encounter. Little did she know that she and her sister would see all sorts of strange and wonderful things over the course of their lives, and they would also become the greatest Dragon Chasers ever, but that is a tale for a different time.

CHAPTER FIVE

THE PREDICAMENT AT POMPEII

So, Bug had managed to escape the *almost* destruction of Atlantis, feeling only marginally guilty that he had been personally responsible for the near collapse of an entire civilisation.

For now, Bug had put the dragons off the scent by declaring that he only had *four* Gems and by swearing, foot on heart, that the last missing Gem was somewhere at the bottom of the ocean. It was a stroke of luck for our Bug that the dragons had no idea how much he fibbed about things. In fact, he fibs so much about *everything* that we have to remember that even this story may not be a totally accurate version of what happened.

After the "Accident at Atlantis", as he had taken to calling it, Bug found himself once again adrift in the sea. For a change, Bug decided to let the sea take him wherever it wanted, and he soon washed up on the shores of Italy, in the small, bustling town of Pompeii, on the volcanic slopes of Mount Vesuvius.

Bug's little eyes lit up when he saw the volcano, smoke gently drifting upwards from the top. Thinking that he had at last found the perfect hiding place for his last Dragon Gem, Bug immediately started climbing the mountain. He was *dripping* with sweat by the time he was halfway up, because Italy was hot enough already without being on the slopes of a massive volcano, but Bug kept going, as he was still convinced it was the ideal safe spot for his last bit of treasure. Just inside the top of the volcano, he found a ledge that seemed *perfect* for hiding his final Dragon Gem. He was just about ready to place the Gem *really carefully* on the

ledge when he slipped, and the Gem fell down into the volcano, heading straight for the boiling lava below.

Bug watched in horror as his beloved treasure landed on a small rock sticking out over the molten lava. He tried to lower himself down into the volcano to grab the Gem, but it was far, far too hot and he had to give up when some of his fuzz got singed.

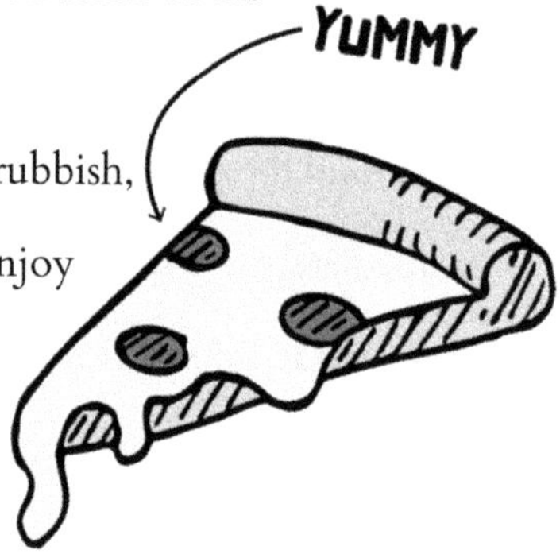

Several hours later, feeling rather rubbish, Bug headed back into the town to enjoy his first proper meal in ages. Not being able to get hold of a cheese and pickle sandwich, he found a little street café that sold delicious-looking pizza by the slice. Once his tummy was full, Bug decided to explore his new surroundings, thinking that he should probably find somewhere to bed down for the night in his little jar. (Having your own home with you at all times is incredibly useful, but he needed to make sure he had somewhere safe to be, as he certainly didn't want to be thrown into the recycling, which had happened before.)

Just as he turned a corner, he bumped into a boy, causing the poor lad to drop an enormous pile of papers he was carrying.

"Oh! *Mi scusi*!" said Bug, and he immediately began to help gather the papers.

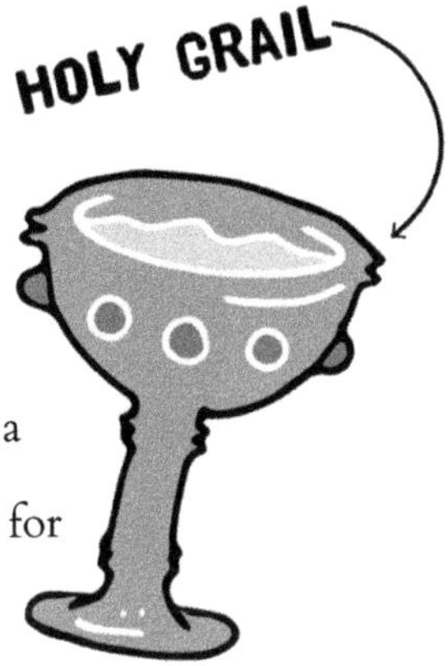

It turned out that the boy, who was called Gino, was headed home, and being a lovely lad, he offered Bug a place to sleep for the night, so that Bug and his jar did not end up in the recycling truck... again.

Bug spent a happy two weeks with Gino and his family, lazing in the sunshine and enjoying good, home-cooked Italian food. In the evenings, the family would sit out on the terrace and Bug would tell them stories from his past, including the tale of how Bug had *temporarily* misplaced the Holy Grail, and how he managed *somehow* to lose the Great Library of Alexandria. I'm not sure Gino's family believed all of the tales Bug told, but they were more than happy to listen and to "ooh" and "ah" in all the right places. Bug was so happy, in fact, that he totally forgot about the Dragon Gem he had dropped in the volcano, which was why it came as quite a surprise when he woke up one

morning to find a huge dragon on the front lawn. Prince Grane had tracked him down. And the dragon was ANGRY.

Prince Grane had landed right in front of Gino's house, dwarfing the villa and terrifying Gino's poor neighbours.

Bug went sheepishly out, to see what he could do to make the dragon go away, but before he had time to do or say anything, the dragon took hold of Bug in his great jaws and shook him angrily.

"*Where* is my last Gem?" growled the dragon, clearly not pleased to be seeing Bug again. (It was also really difficult to speak with Bug in his mouth. I would imagine that Prince Grane was a bit embarrassed by how muffled he sounded, and I have to say that it ruined the effect a bit, if I'm honest.)

"I lost it," replied Bug, at last actually telling the truth. "I dropped it in the volcano but…" Before Bug had time to finish his sentence, the great white dragon flew off towards the volcano, the wind from his enormous wings covering Pompeii with ash.

Bug quickly signalled to Gino and his family to run to their fishing boat, which they reached just in time. You see, the dragon easily reclaimed his Dragon Gem (as dragons and fire go hand-in-hand) but unfortunately, the beating of the dragon's wings did more than just cover the town with ash.

Bug joined Gino on his family's boat and made amends by pointing them in the direction of Atlantis and his friends there. He knew that Gino would make a good pal for Alice and Elizabeth, and that Katarina would make sure they were safe and looked after. Once they were safely on their way, Bug hopped off the side of the boat, leaving yet another scene of chaos and carnage in his wake, and set off on another adventure.

CHAPTER SIX

THE PICKLE PROBLEM

After these two total disasters, Bug decided to lay low for a while. *In fact*, Bug thought, *I could do with a holiday.* Not fancying another seaside town, as they appeared to be unlucky, Bug emailed his old friend Derek, who lived in a small cave off the coast of Nova Scotia. Derek and Bug went *way* back. It was important for Derek to live in a cave and not, say, in a house, like normal people, because Derek *isn't a normal person.* In fact, he isn't a person at all, normal or otherwise. He's a little purple **ALIEN**. A very cute one, mind, not a scary one.

As soon as Bug arrived, however, there was a change of

plan. Unfortunately, Derek had received a call from his mum asking him to go home and fix the internet. Bug was very disappointed by this news, as it had been a long time since Bug and Derek had had a proper catch-up. But then Bug had an idea. He could go along too! An off-world vacation would be just the ticket.

The flight took around four hours, but luckily Derek had planned plenty of in-flight entertainment, as he knew that Bug had the attention span of a gnat. The time flew by! Bug was only bored twice, and even that was short-lived, as Derek had given him a tablet on which he could watch cartoons.

Once Derek had nipped home to check on his mum (it turned out the router just needed turning off and on again) he was free to show Bug around his homeworld.

Derek's planet was dry and barren except for three huge rivers that were filled with lush green plants. The green plants were what Derek's species ate. They harvested the plants to make this weird, smelly green mush that they served in bowls and ate with big wooden spoons. Derek had made a special bowl of mush for Bug to try, but after a first taste, Bug couldn't say that he was massively impressed.

Derek also took Bug into the mountains to see the lake where all the rivers started. They took a picnic with them, as it was quite a long trip, and Derek knew that Bug would be hungry by the time they got there. Bug had decided not to eat the green mush any more, so instead he had packed a cheese and pickle sandwich for himself. Bug really liked the lake and the mountains, as this part of the planet was very green with pretty red flowers all around. Derek was enjoying showing Bug where he lived, as he hadn't been able to bring anyone home in a long time. As you probably already know, not everyone can withstand deep space travel. (In fact, Derek had discovered that humans *in particular* are really, really awful at it. It's probably best not to ask how he found this out.)

So Derek and Bug were enjoying a picnic on the side of the beautiful lake that fed the plant-rich rivers. At this point, I

will have to admit that Bug and I have something in common – we occasionally stop listening when people are talking to us. Does that happen to you? When people start going on and on about things that I'm not massively interested in, I find my mind wandering to such questions as, "If cats had opposable thumbs, would they rule the world rather than humans?" And other such day-to-day musings.

Derek had just gotten to the point about the delicate ecosystem on his planet, and how carefully it had to be maintained, when Bug started thinking quite carefully about the colour purple. In fact, he was thinking about it so much that he *totally missed* what Derek said next. When Bug tuned back in, his little heart almost stopped.

"Did you just say 'nothing must enter the lake'?"

"That's right," said Derek. "It is **MASSIVELY** important that the lake is **COMPLETELY UNDISTURBED**, otherwise, there would be a **DISASTER OF MIGHTY PROPORTIONS**." He was quite clear about it all.

"Oh," said Bug, very, very quietly.

Derek started to go a little pale. Which was difficult as he was quite a pale shade of lavender to begin with. (Maybe because he had been on Earth and hadn't been eating the right amount of green mush? Just a thought.)

"Bug?" Derek asked quietly, dread filling his heart (which was in his left foot). "What did you do?"

"I *may have* thrown a *tiny* bit of my cheese and pickle sandwich to a fish I saw." Bug went even quieter. "The fish was in the lake," he added, in case he hadn't been clear enough.

WELL OF COURSE THE FISH WAS IN THE LAKE WHERE ELSE WOULD IT HAVE BEEN ??!??

Bug could tell that Derek was perhaps a little upset. "Funny you should ask," began Bug, "because I once saw a fish..."

"Be *quiet*!" Derek cut him off before he had even finished the sentence. "Get back to my ship, NOW. I need to get you off-planet before you cause any more damage, and before people find out what you've done!"

For once, Bug did as he was told. He turned tail and headed straight back down the mountain. The path ran right by the river, and as he was scarpering as fast as he could, he noticed a black, inky stain starting to spread through the water.

"Derek, what is that?"

"*That*," replied Derek, "is what happens when you put a cheese and pickle sandwich in the lake!"

Bug watched in horror as the black stain reached the lush green plants. They too turned black, then withered, then shrivelled, then vanished below the now thick, dark waters of the river.

Bug hung his head as he watched *ALL* the plants die. "Well," he thought. "Now I've done it."

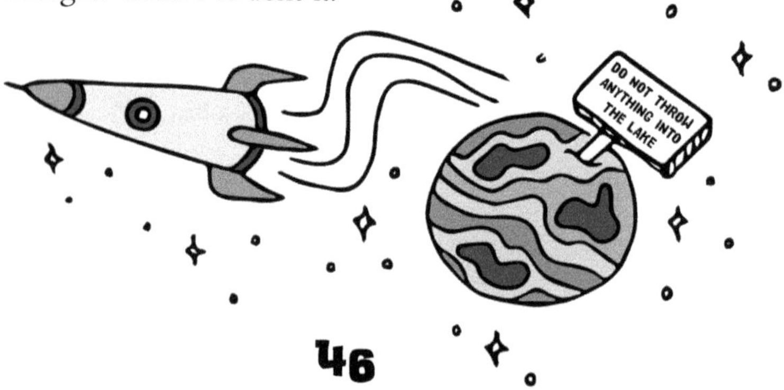

CHAPTER SEVEN

DEREK DESERVES A MENTION

As Bug watches the food source of an entire alien world die because of his carelessness, I thought I might take the opportunity to tell you a bit more about Derek, as I feel you haven't been properly introduced.

Derek first came to Earth many years into the future. Now that might sound a little strange, until you realise that Derek's spacecraft is not only capable of passing through galaxies but also passing through *time itself*. And one of the reasons that Bug and Derek get on so well is that Derek can *also* be a bit of a troublemaker. Not quite to the same extent as Bug, but he has certainly had his moments.

Derek's spacecraft first landed on Earth in America in 1947, in a little town called Roswell. Now this caused a bit of a stir, as quite a few people were watching when Derek lost control of his ship and crash-landed in the desert. I'm not sure if you know this story or not, but here it is from Derek's side.

Derek was flying back to Earth after spending Christmas with his family on his homeworld (Derek's species celebrate Christmas in June), when he thought he would pop down to his favourite diner for a coffee. Like most of his species, Derek loved the green mush, but he was also fond of a skinny latte with soy milk. Distracted for a minute by a passing shooting star, he typed in the wrong date on his control panel, and instead of nineteen *ninety*-seven, he hit nineteen *forty*-seven - which was totally no good, as skinny lattes with soy milk hadn't even been invented in nineteen *forty*-seven. Even worse, because of the wrong date, Derek's favourite coffee shop had also not been invented yet, and this was most confusing to Derek, who hadn't noticed his error. And because Derek was looking so carefully for the specific coffee shop that he liked the most, he didn't see the

lamp post straight ahead of him. Rather embarrassingly, Derek clipped the top of the lamp post, sending his craft into a spin that he couldn't control. Derek landed with a bump on the edge of the desert, much to the shock of several witnesses, and a couple of lizards who had paused to catch their breath after a fairly long early-morning run.

For a couple of minutes, Derek was a bit shaken. He did a quick check of himself and his craft and noted a fairly big bump on his head and a small crack on the ship's control panel. Derek sighed. He would need a few minutes to sort out the crack, as it had unfortunately gone right through the on/off button, and *this* meant that his ship couldn't fly.

Within ten seconds, **THREE BLACK CARS** had pulled up outside, and within a further thirty seconds, a tent had gone up all around him and his craft. Thankful for some privacy, and a chance to catch his breath, Derek climbed gingerly out, still feeling a little dizzy from the spin.

"Are you okay, sir?" There was a man dressed all in black, wearing

sunglasses, which was rather silly as they were now inside the tent.

Derek peered at the man carefully. "Ah, John, it's you! How's the wife?" Derek was relieved to see a Government Agent that he had met several times before.

John frowned. "Well, I'm not actually married, sir," he replied.

Realisation dawned. "Err…What's the date today?" asked Derek.

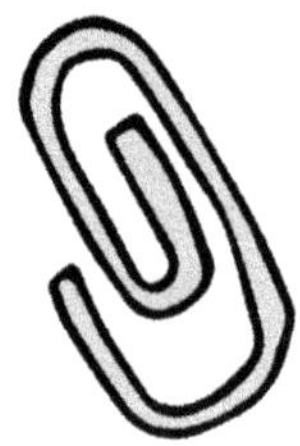

"June 15th, 1947, sir."

"Oh, bother. That explains the missing coffee shop! Now, when you meet your wife next week, make sure to say 'hello' from me and let her know that I would be delighted to come for tea on the tenth. Next year, that is. "

John was now totally confused. "Er, thank you, sir. Do you need assistance to get back on your way?"

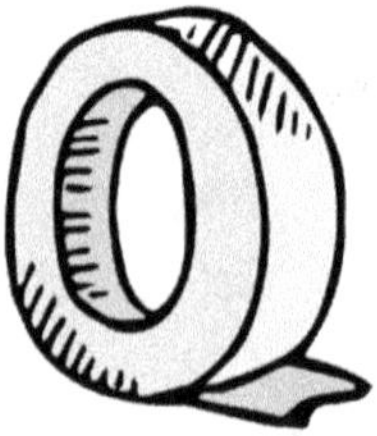

"Yes. That would be wonderful. I could do with a paperclip, two rolls of Sellotape, and a rubber duck."

John masked his surprise beautifully. "Yes, sir. Right away."

John scarpered off to his vehicle and, after a mere five minutes, had gathered all the supplies that Derek had asked for. Now, John had only recently joined the special government agency that aided Intergalactic Alien Travellers, so he couldn't help but ask, "Sir, if I may, what is the rubber duck for?"

Derek smiled and shook his head gravely. "If you have to ask, John, you'll never know."

Derek ducked his head under the doorway and disappeared into his craft, and after five minutes of banging and crashing, all was well.

"Sorry about that, chaps," Derek said to the agents. "I undershot the time. You don't know when skinny lattes will be invented, do you? No? Oh well, never mind. Thanks for the help!" (Aliens, in my experience, are almost always incredibly polite. They rarely forget their pleases and thank yous.)

With that, Derek pressed the "on" button on his control panel and it all lit up happily. Derek was once again surrounded by the familiar bleeps, bloops and flashes. A nod of the head to John, and Derek was off, barely hearing John and his colleagues explaining to surprised onlookers that a weather balloon had just come crashing down and they were going to take it back to the air base around the corner.

CHAPTER EIGHT

THE LOST LIBRARY OF ALEXANDRIA

Did I ever tell you how I met our mischievous Bug in the first place? It's a good story (even if I do say so myself), so I don't think you'll mind me sharing it. In fact, it also covers another of Bug's tales that we mentioned back in Italy - The Lost Library of Alexandria.

Now, the Lost Library is an interesting story in itself, but it gets even more interesting when you add Bug into the mix. It all started when I was visiting the pyramids of Egypt, just after they were built. Now you obviously know that the pyramids were built by aliens (because, really, what other plausible explanation is there?), but did you know it was actually *Derek* who was the lead architect on the project? That means that Derek was the one who drew up all the plans and built the little scale models that you see on the telly. (It's actually interesting to note that the pyramids were, at one point, going to be significantly *smaller* than they are today. Not by design, but because Derek knocked over his soy latte on the plans, ruining the drawings and covering over the measurements. So instead of being 139 *metres* tall (as they are today), they would have been 13.9 *centimetres* tall, so they could have stood on your desk at school. Needless to say, someone *then* had to be employed to make sure Derek was properly reading his own plans. After this small incident, The Pyramid Project progressed nicely. Anyway. I digress. Again.)

So there I was, admiring the finishing touches that were being applied to the pyramids, when this little fluffball appeared beside me.

"Hello!" I said, surprised.

"Mmmpfff," said Bug.

"I'm sorry, I didn't quite catch that."

"Mmmpfff!"

I was about to move away, slowly, like you would do if you had just discovered someone who seemed entirely mad, but something about him caught my attention.

"MMMPFFF!"

"Oh!" I said, realisation dawning. "I see! Here, stand still and let me help."

You see, Bug had been eating toffee and it had got stuck in his fur, effectively gluing his mouth shut. (If I had known more about him at the time, I might have been tempted to leave him like that. At least life would have been quieter.)

Once I had freed him from his toffee prison, we introduced ourselves properly. Bug explained that his good friend Derek was in charge of building the pyramids, and he was simply waiting around until he finished for the day so they could go and get a nice dinner.

I have to say that the pyramids really were (and are) astonishing. (At the time, they were all white and shiny, which I

BOOKS IN THE LOST LIBRARY

think is the main reason that Bug wanted to be there. In fact, I have a sneaking suspicion that Bug being in Egypt wasn't so much about meeting Derek as seeing the shiny bits on top of the pyramids.)

Bug and I got to talking and he told me all about the Library at Alexandria. Have you heard of it? Well, its location was a closely guarded secret, and for some reason unknown and unknowable, someone in charge had given Bug responsibility for looking after the map. (This person was clearly an idiot, and I'm sure, by now, they know it too.) Now the library contained hundreds and hundreds *and hundreds* of *really important* documents, from books of medicine to information about dragons and ghosts and werewolves and such, and I had *always* wanted to visit. After talking to Bug for a little bit, I asked (rather cheekily) if he wouldn't mind taking a trip to Alexandria (which wasn't too far from the pyramids) so that I could take a sneakypeeky at the Library.

It was then that I learned what had happened, and why the library is now referred to as "The Lost Library". You see, one of Bug's adventures had taken him (for some reason, I am unclear about why) to Antarctica, and it would appear that the map to the Library had slipped out of his bag, and was now somewhere in the Antarctic Ocean.

"You lost the map?" I asked him, I admit, somewhat incredulously.

Bug nodded. "I didn't *mean* to…"

"But surely there must be another map? And isn't an enormous building filled with books, I don't know, obvious?"

Bug shook his head. "It's underground."

"Oh," I said. "And where is the entrance?"

"Can't remember," answered Bug, most unhelpfully (and totally not bothered, by the way).

"And is there no way to find the entrance?"

Bug shook his head again. "I hid it. Under the sand. And I

forgot to put an 'X'."

I think this was the *exact moment* that I understood what being Bug's friend would mean. "So you hid the entrance to the most important building in the *whole world*, and then lost the only map that shows how to find it?"

"Yep," said Bug, quite nonchalantly. "Fancy a sandwich?"

I sighed. "Go on, then. Why not?" I sat down on the sand, and I knew from that moment on, Bug and I would be firm friends.

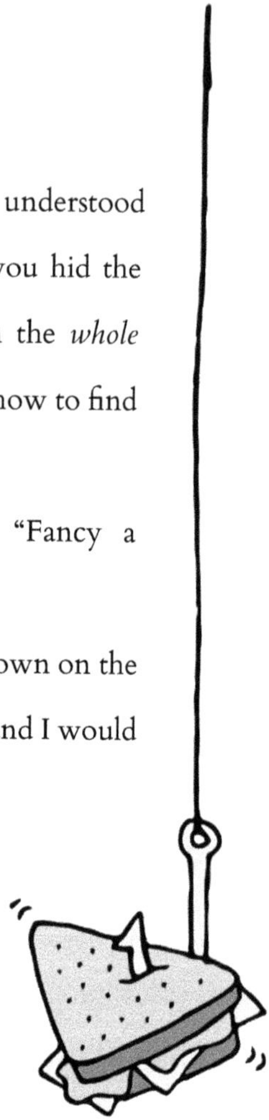

CHAPTER NINE

THE LADY OF THE LAKE

Anyway, back to Bug's adventures in space. So this final story is actually one where Bug comes out quite well. I know, surprising, right?

Having successfully run away from Derek's planet, (I know I keep calling it that, but otherwise, I would have to keep typing "**PBJADFJLHGAELYUFQH;WLKEFN M,XN SBHG CFW1EYTDGQW;QWNGRKJR563BNEGV,JBVWHG EFYWWCE'NJHAV';AGRPUI05B OB**", and who has the time for that?) Derek's spaceship touched down in England in an unknown time and place. This is because Derek's control panel had never really recovered from the Roswell crash, and he was too embarrassed to go and ask for another one. But anyway, it made for some quite exciting adventures, never knowing where you were going to end up.

Derek's spaceship touched down in the middle of a field, startling some nearby sheep. (It was a bit foggy out, so Bug and Derek couldn't *really* see where they had landed anyway.) Glad of a spot of fresh air, they climbed out of the spaceship. Because it was misty, Bug's fuzz started to curl up, as it does when it is wet. Bug was a bit annoyed about this, as he had spent quite a lot of the flight straightening it with Derek's mum's hair straighteners.

He soon shrugged off annoyance though, as he didn't want a bit of mist to ruin his good mood. (Our Bug has an amazing way to bounce back. He'd totally destroyed several places by this point, but he wasn't going to let *that* bring him down.) They walked a little way, very carefully, because they couldn't even see their hands in front of their faces, the fog was so thick. ("A proper pea-souper", my Gran would have called it.) And it was a good job they were walking carefully, too, because otherwise they would have ended up very soggy indeed, not just a little damp.

"A lake!" exclaimed Bug.

"Don't you dare throw anything in!" warned Derek, who was still a little sore about the whole 'Pickle Problem'.

"Fancy a swim, Derek?"

"I do not, thank you."

Derek's tone of voice made our Bug think that his friend might still be a little put out.

Bug didn't get chance to swim, however, because just as he was about to dip his big toe in, they heard a loud, booming voice...

WHO DARES ENTER THE LAKE?

Bug and Derek looked at each other.

I SAID,
WHO IS IT THAT
DARES TO ENTER THE

LAKE?

Bug and Derek stayed quiet.

ANSWER, OR FOREVER BE
DOO

MTED!

"Er… *me*?" ventured Bug.

"Bug! Oh, sorry, love, it's you. Just give me a sec."

Derek looked at Bug, who was bouncing up and down excitedly, when suddenly, a beautiful woman broke through the surface of the lake.

"By 'eck, Bug, it's good to see you!"

Bug ran into the water and gave the woman a soggy cuddle. "Derek, it's Viviane! Come and say hello!"

"Er, hello?" said Derek, a little cautiously, as not everyone responded well to seeing a little green alien. But Viviane barely paused when she saw him standing on the shoreline. She was a mystical being herself, after all.

"Hi, Derek," Viviane waved. "Soz for the theatricals. Gotta keep strangers away from the lake. It's dead magical and stuff. You know how it is."

Slightly bemused, Derek watched as the beautiful woman chatted away quite happily with Bug. Whilst they were busy in conversation, Derek had a little wander around and found an information sign by a tree. Now, Derek can't read English, but I can, so this is what it said:

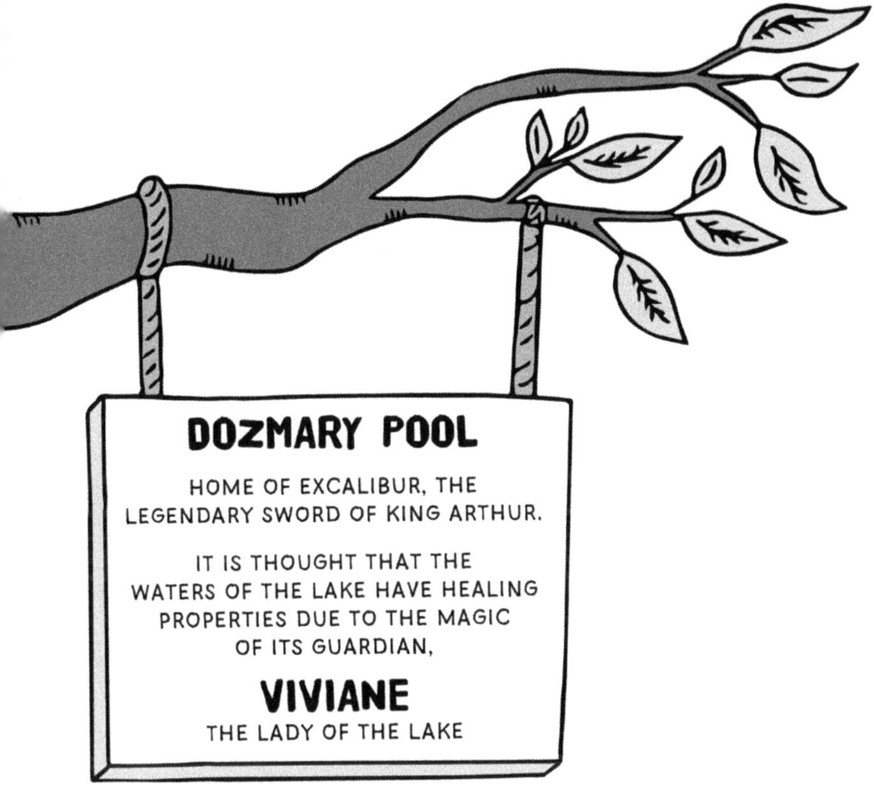

Derek returned to Bug and Viviane, an idea forming in his mind. As he approached, he just caught the tail end of the conversation.

Viviane was wagging a finger at Bug. "Now, be honest, naughty Bug, because the last time I saw Excalibur, *YOU* had it and you had *promised* to take it *straight* to Arthur. But you didn't show up at the castle for three months! Arthur told me! Now. *Where did you go?*"

Bug looked down at his feet, which was a little difficult, as they were underwater.

"I got it stuck."

"Stuck? Where? How?" Viviane frowned, not quite understanding yet.

"I'm not really sure *how*," replied Bug. "But it was in a …. well, it was in a sort of *stone* for a while."

Viviane laughed. "Oh for goodness sake. That was *you?*"

Bug nodded and Viviane rubbed his fuzz on the top of his head. "You do get into scrapes, don't you?"

Bug smiled, all innocence, whilst he enjoyed being fussed by his friend. In fact, he was enjoying his head rubs so much that he started to rumble and grumble, which is Bug's way of purring. Within a minute, his leg started twitching, too. Just like a dog when you find the sweet spot on his tummy.

As Derek approached, Bug and Viviane turned to look at him.

"Bug! I think I may have found an answer to the problem on

PBJADFJLHGAELYUFQH;WLKEFN M,XN SBHGCF W1EYTDGQW;QWNGRKJR563BNEGV,JBVWHGEFY

WWCE'NJHAV';AGRPUIO5B OB." (Okay, I tried it, and it's ridiculous. I'm going back to "homeworld".)

Bug looked up, semi-hopefully. In all truth, he wasn't actually too bothered about the rest of the aliens, but he wasn't keen on Derek being cross with him.

"Viviane," asked Derek, "would you mind taking a trip back to my homeworld?" (See, it works *so* much better.)

Bug started to realise what Derek was thinking. "Viviane! You could fix the lake!" He bounced up and down on his toes with excitement.

After Viviane had heard the tale of the Pickle Problem, she readily agreed, happy to help. (She is good people, after all.)

She thought for a moment about what to pack, and then decided on bringing nothing at all, which to be honest, I quite admire. In fact, I respect anyone who manages to pack light. I've never managed it.

"Let me just hang my sign up and I'll be right with you,." she told them.

She dived under the water and came back up with a *Gone to Lunch, Back Soon* sign, which she hung on a tree branch.

"Right," said Derek. "It'll be a bit of a squeeze, but let's go fix the lake!"

Bug smiled happily. Derek was back to being his normal cheerful self, and Bug was getting to spend a bit longer with Viviane, who he hadn't seen in forever.

As the three of them headed back off to Derek's homeworld (yes, definitely the right decision) Bug felt quite content. Thanks to his friendship with the Lady of the Lake, Derek's food source would be restored and *all in all*, he thought, *that's a happy ending.*

In fact, Bug was so happy about how neatly everything had turned out, that his mind started to wander to new adventures, and we all know what that leads to. *Trouble.*

But, lovely human readers, I'm afraid that Bug's next mishaps will have to wait until another time. My hand has cramped up with all this typing and writing, and I quite fancy a cheese-and-pickle myself. I can promise, though, that this is not the end of Bug's adventures, and I have already promised *him* that I will write the next lot down after I have had a long, peaceful, well-deserved and uninterrupted holiday. Although I think I will steer clear of anywhere Bug has been for a little while, you know, just to let the dust settle. And in case you were wondering what happened to Bug's pals (like Harry, Gino, the Dragon Chasers and even the (potential) pirates), don't worry. They'll be back.

Ooh… did I just hear that someone put the kettle on? *Lovely*. Two sugars in mine, please.

TO BE CONTINUED….

P.S. I've always wanted to write that. It sounds super dramatic, don't you think?

TURN THE PAGE TO READ A SNEAK PEAK OF BUG'S NEXT ADVENTURE!

PREVIEW OF

THE MYSTERIOUS LIFE & TIMES OF BUG

VOLUME 2

Now. Do you remember the two (potential) pirates from the story of the Stolen Gems? (You seem like you're really clever, so I bet you do.) Well, they're back. And they're cross. Oh, and I should also tell you that in the time since the Great Gem Heist, Bug had come to the conclusion, (after much thought), that they were probably and most definitely pirates, so I feel okay referring to them as such for the rest of this story.

So Bug had left the island with the stolen Gems, (having left a note to tell the dragons exactly where he was headed), but there were also the birds that had been nicking the treasure as well, remember? The birds, you see, were like magpies, and they also loved the shiny things that they had found in the chest. Before long, their nests were lined with the most dazzling diamond rings and necklaces, quite enough to make anyone jealous. But… what I haven't told you yet is that the pirates, you see, were part of Blackbeard's crew, and if you don't know who Blackbeard is, then hold on to your hat, because he was the nastiest, meanest pirate in the whole wide world. And the treasure the pair of pirates had been hiding, was actually his. Oops.

I'm not sure how the conversation went, because Bug wasn't there for this part, but I would imagine it went something like this.

"Oi, Wazzock," said Pirate One.

"Will you please stop calling me that? I'll tell your mum if you don't," answered Wazzock.

(I should point out that they were fully grown pirates, but who isn't scared of their mum when they're in trouble?)

"Where did we put the treasure? I can't see the 'X'," said Pirate One.

(We really could do with knowing his name.)

"Well, I don't know. You were the one in charge of the

digging," said Wazzock.

"Who said?" asked Pirate One (this is getting silly now).

"You said, you great lump of lard!"

(Ah ha!)

"I didn't!" said Great Lump of Lard.

This conversation (likely) went back and forth for a while before Bug appeared on the shoreline, fancying himself a little bit of sunbathing. Noticing the pirates, he hid in the shallows, waiting until they went away. They would absolutely spoil his peace and quiet, which after his last adventure, he sorely needed.

I'm not sure if you know this already, but Bug often returns to places he has been before, which is why he has so many friends, and he quite fancied having a little chat with the birds. He was also hoping that they might be kind enough to break open one of those coconutty-things that they seemed so fond of.

But running into the pair of pirates was the last thing that Bug wanted. And they were taking

AAAAAAGGES.

ABOUT THE AUTHOR

KATE is a writer of stories, poems, tales, and other English words. Kate believes that children's imaginations should be kept alive as long as possible and so, at the age of 42, she has made the brave decision not to grow any older, to ensure her own imagination stays active.

When not writing the best stories in the entire world, Kate plays piano, walks on mountains, and sometimes skis down them, too. Her life is filled with plants, pets, fun and frolics in the home she shares with her husband, children and step-children. Oh, and her Mum, who lives next door. **(SORRY MUM... NEARLY FORGOT).**

www.ingramcontent.com/pod-product-compliance
Ingram Content Group UK Ltd.
Pitfield, Milton Keynes, MK11 3LW, UK
UKHW020805070425
5351UKWH00031B/367

9 781068 309908